The Way of the Wealthy Woman

WRITTEN BY TAYLOR EATON

DESIGNED BY STEPHANIE WICKER-CAMPBELL
EDITED BY BAYLEE FOX

MUSE
ORACLE
PRESS

PUBLISHED BY MUSE ORACLE PRESS PTY LTD

The Way of the Wealthy Woman™ Journal

ISBN: 978-0-6458850-8-8

Published by Muse Oracle Press Pty Ltd, 2024.

The Way of the Wealthy Woman Journal - Inspiration, Practices, and Wisdom to Activate Abundance

Author: Taylor Eaton
Designer: Stephanie Wicker-Campbell
Editor: Baylee Fox

The Way of The Wealthy Woman

"The Wealthy Woman is rich in ways that are too numerous to count.

She is rich in her love for herself. She knows her worth. She trusts in the inevitable flow of money. And because she trusts so deeply, she feels wealthy at all times.

It is because she feels wealthy that money flows to her. Not the other way around."

INDEX

INDEX

DEDICATION

For my daughter, Ramona, who is an infinite wealth of laughter, joy, and love.

The Wealthy Woman Oracle Deck

While this journal is a powerful tool for financial transformation on its own, I created it to work in harmony with The Wealthy Woman Oracle Deck. The deck will provide you with guidance and clarity along your journey to prosperity, whereas this journal will help you dive deep into the inner work that will make your journey easier. Use the deck and journal together for the most magical and meaningful results.

You can find The Wealthy Woman Oracle Deck by scanning the QR code below.

Activation Audios

Throughout this journal are several activations for abundance. You can access audio recordings of these activations at www.tayloreaton.com/wealthywomanactivations

INTRODUCTION

In a world brimming with immeasurable possibilities, there exist countless paths that one can take to achieve wealth. But not all paths are created equal. Some are rocky and steep, making the journey to abundance feel arduous and insurmountable. Other paths are long and tiring, with endless pitfalls that instill doubt or fear. Yet other paths require an unsustainable pace and personal sacrifice, leaving the traveler wondering if the reward will be worth the journey. Of the many paths to prosperity that exist, most that have been laid out and traversed by others are unenjoyable—and often unproductive—to walk. They leave those who travel them feeling exhausted, resentful, or lacking in finances and a multitude of other ways.

There is a path that offers a different option, a road that deviates from the traditional teachings of struggle as a means to riches. Embarking on this journey allows self-trust and self-love to act as the driving forces that propel oneself toward abundance. You will discover the philosophy that money can come easily and the journey to it can be just as rewarding as the financial prize itself —an approach to creating true wealth on all levels: spiritual, mental, emotional, and material. This path is *The Way of the Wealthy Woman*.

A Journey to True Wealth

The Way of the Wealthy Woman provides a nurturing approach to looking at money and our relationship with it. It invites us to explore the most tender, powerful, and sacred parts of ourselves to create wealth that reflects those qualities in our lives. Having more money than you know what to do with won't serve you if the way you have to obtain or continually manage that money is unenjoyable, unsustainable, or laden with fear.

Money, after all, does not change us or our circumstances. It only amplifies who we have become and what we have cultivated within our lives on our way to it.

You do not need to identify as a woman to benefit from the teachings of *The Way of the Wealthy Woman*, for this message seeks to activate the soft—yet strong—feminine energy that we all carry within us so that it can be applied to money (and all forms of abundance) for ultimate ease and growth. *The Way of the Wealthy Woman* is for anyone looking for a more feminine approach to money that puts your own well-being and empowerment at the forefront. This way is for those who have trodden the traditional routes to money and come up short or disenchanted. This way is for those who seek true wealth—the fulfillment, enjoyment, and generosity of money—not just the acquisition of it. The truth is that you have the innate power to shape your financial reality with your thoughts, energy, and actions. In order to harness this power to create the abundance you desire in your life, you must know how to access it.

The Way of the Wealthy Woman teaches this to those who choose to walk it.

The Wealthy Woman's approach to abundance will appear to you when you are ready to embrace its teachings. Trust that you are not reading these words by mistake or coincidence. If this message has found its way into your life, it is meant for you to hear. You are ready.

The principles behind *The Way of the Wealthy Woman* appeared in my life at a time when I most needed them. Fresh out of college, education and living costs buried me in six figures of debt.

So, I did exactly what I had been taught to do and had done my whole life up until that point: I buckled down, worked hard, and sacrificed my peace of mind in the quest for financial stability. I was playing by all the rules I'd been taught about success and money. I was focused, logical, and highly driven. Yet, even after landing a full-time job, being promoted at an astonishing rate, praised, and given multiple raises, I still wasn't being paid enough to pay more than the bare minimum of my living expenses and bills.

I felt as though I would never get to where I wanted to be financially. I would be hustling and burning myself out for decades to make ends meet. Even worse, I ended up with this crushing amount of debt by doing everything "right": studying hard, graduating from college with the highest marks possible, and being an employee who went above and beyond. I had played by the rules I'd been taught my whole life. I'd done what I was *supposed* to do to make money. Yet there I was with debilitating debt, no money to travel or do the things I wanted to do, and no hope for anything to change on the horizon. That was when I realized that the "rules" we're given around money aren't necessarily correct. I started looking outside the typical financial advice of *hard work* and *budgeting* and delved deep into my relationship with money and, therefore, my relationship with myself. I saw some shifts in my income, some miraculous leaps, and manifestations. But I still felt limited.

This yearning to find a different approach to money—one that would actually yield the life of freedom and stability that I wanted—was pushed into further clarity when my father fell terminally ill. This encounter with loss left me devastated, raw, and acutely aware of my own mortality. That was the moment I finally threw out any last rules around money that I was clinging to.

I started trusting my intuition instead of what I had been told I needed to do to make money. I began doing what I loved without waiting for it to make *logical* sense to do so. I shifted my measure of success from one of financial gain to one of living a fulfilled life. I started valuing the unique gifts and skills I had that society had told me would never be lucrative.

I started a business. I left my job. I dove deep into spirituality, mindset, and manifestation so that I could apply those principles to money. I broke all the rules of what I was supposed to do to be wealthy. Within a year and a half of starting my business, I scaled it to bring in six figures. That, paired with other miraculous manifestations, meant that I had gone from $100,000 in debt to over $100,000 in the bank.

My success grew exponentially from there, and my business has now allowed me to help thousands of others shift their financial reality. I did this all by focusing on the following things:

1. *Healing* **my limiting beliefs** around money that kept me on a path that didn't allow me to ever reach my financial desires.
2. **Cultivating deep** *trust* **in myself** (so that I could listen to and act on my inner guidance) and in the universe (so that I could release what I couldn't control and focus on what I could).
3. **Connecting with my innate** *worthiness* (so that I could allow myself to want to be wealthy, receive money without shame, and leverage my most powerful money-making gifts that would have otherwise been left untapped).
4. **Learning how to hold the** *vision* **of my desires** (so I could feel wealthy and successful before the money showed up, thus becoming magnetic to people, opportunities, and money itself).

As I mastered these key areas on deeper and deeper levels over the years (and taught them to countless others who thrived with them), I found that they activated something sacred within me. Every time I worked on these concepts within myself, a new version of myself emerged: a part of me that society and my conditioning had shoved aside for decades, a part of me that was nurturing, gentle, and loving, yet strong, powerful, and fearless. My inner Wealthy Woman became more and more activated until I finally let her take the lead and guide me to more abundance and fulfillment than I ever dreamed was possible.

And so, *The Way of the Wealthy Woman* was born.

This approach to money has objectively and miraculously changed my financial reality, but more importantly—it has profoundly changed *me*.

I am so grateful for all that I have learned on this journey. I am honored to share this journal to help guide you through these four key elements that will allow you to journey to abundance in *The Way of the Wealthy Woman.*

UNLOCKING THE POWER
OF THIS JOURNAL

This journal is so incredibly powerful and versatile. The prompts in this journal are different from your standard prompts that barely scratch the surface of your money stories or financial reality. This journal's content is divided into four sections, each focusing on one of the key elements of the Wealthy Woman's teachings.

You are welcome to go through the journal in sequential order. But you are also welcome to randomly flip through the journal and stop wherever your intuition guides you to stop, trusting that whatever message, image, quote, exercise, or prompt you land on is exactly what you need at that moment. Use the journal at whatever pace feels right to you. The work you will do in this journal and the transformation you will undergo is sacred, deep work. Do not rush through it. Take your time. Be gentle and loving with yourself as you go through this metamorphosis.

The more intentional you become, the greater shifts in your financial reality you will make possible. If you should uncover anything along the way that feels too heavy or irresponsible for you to transmute on your own, be sure to seek out professional assistance.

Honor Your Path

I encourage you to shape your experience with this

journal in whatever way feels best to you. If exercises or prompts don't resonate with you, skip them. If you feel the need to revisit the same section five times over to feel like you've gotten what you need from it, allow yourself to do so. If the term Universe (or anything else) isn't your preferred terminology, replace it in your mind —or even on the page—with Source, God, Goddess, Love, The Divine, Higher Self, Energy, or whatever you please.

Always trust what feels right to you (that's one of the core teachings here, after all!). We are all unique with different experiences with money, different financial desires, and at different parts of our journey to wealth. Honor your unique path.

Amplify Your Results

The teachings presented in this journal first came through as an oracle deck titled *The Wealthy Woman Oracle Deck*. I created the deck as a tool to detach from the traditional rules around money that have kept so many of us stuck and disempowered for far too long so we could instead tune into more healing, trust, worthiness, and embodiment around money. This deck has helped me and many others tap into the guidance needed to walk our unique paths to abundance. The art, quotes, and underlying teachings in this journal are pulled from *The Wealthy Woman Oracle Deck*. I have also included instructions for card spreads throughout the journal that are designed specifically for use with

The Wealthy Woman Oracle Deck. These are particularly useful for uncovering any guidance you need when you are uncertain of how to apply your deep work throughout the journal to your life.

Of course, you can use this journal without *The Wealthy Woman Oracle Deck*—it is incredibly powerful and transformative in its own right. But if you want to tap into another level of clarity, trust, and alignment with money, get a copy of *The Wealthy Woman Oracle Deck.* You can scan the code below to do so.

A Blessing for Your Journey

As you set out to embark upon walking in *The Way of the Wealthy Woman*, I offer these words to bless you and your path.

May every step you take along the way
Be illuminated by love and purpose.

May you let this journey to wealth shape you
Into the person you wish to be.

May you know the effortless flow of money
And all the good it can do.

May you always know your true, abundant nature,
As vast and infinite as the cosmos.
For you are both the power that creates abundance…
And abundance itself.

HEALING

"Anything that is healed is only healed as a by-product of love. The more you can give love to yourself, the more you will be moved to take new actions that lead to new fortunes."

The first step on the journey to abundance is one of healing.

The Wealthy Woman does not ignore her wounds or bypass the attention her soul is calling for. She nurtures herself, tending to the things begging to be healed, releasing that which does not support her as she moves toward the wealth she desires.

Gracefully, she examines and addresses all stories, beliefs, habits, and fears she has that may create pitfalls along the path to prosperity. She knows that in doing so, she not only unblocks the natural flow of abundance that is trying to reach her but also lightens her load, making room for new beliefs and ways of being that will get her to the abundance she seeks much faster. As she heals, she gives herself love, celebrating herself for her willingness to look inward and change that which is no longer serving her.

The Wealthy Woman sees the beauty and strength in healing—and she embraces it with an air of sacred reverence and curiosity for what she may uncover, release, and make space for.

Healing As The First Step to Abundance

Healing can be intimidating, for it requires courage and a desire to grow in the direction of your dreams. But it is wildly rewarding in long-term results and often offers immediate clarity, relief, and renewal.

Once you can name your blocks around money, you begin to understand where your relationship with abundance (or yourself) can be strengthened. From there, you can begin to make changes within yourself and your life rather than feeling powerless to influence the ebb and flow of money in your life.

As you embark on this healing phase of your journey, know that you do not need to be perfect or fully healed to call more wealth into your life. Rather, this is something you will dive deeper into and revisit over time as you reach greater and greater levels of prosperity.

This section contains questions, mantras, and exercises to guide you through identifying and healing whatever needs to be released or transmuted to access the money you desire more easily.

Journey through this section, and remember to revisit it as needed—especially if you feel disconnected from the material in later sections of this journal. In that case, come back here to uncover what is waiting to be healed or shifted before you move further down your path to prosperity.

You may find that certain stories may need to be healed, or your perspective around money may need to shift multiple times before it truly sticks. Addressing the same block multiple times is normal and part of your ongoing expansion into more and more abundance.

As you do this sacred healing work, celebrate yourself for the strength and courage it takes to willingly look inward and release what does not support your expansion into more abundance.

CARD SPREADS

HEALING CLARITY CARD SPREAD

Identify What Needs to Be Healed

If, at any point on your journey to more abundance, you feel blocked or stuck and unsure why, use the card spread below to illuminate what needs to be healed or shifted.

This card spread is designed specifically for use with The Wealthy Woman Oracle Deck but can be adapted for other decks.

Instructions:

1. Shuffle your deck while holding the following question in your mind: "What am I now ready to heal in order to strengthen my relationship with money?"
2. Pull three cards, placing them in the provided configuration.
3. Use the guide below to interpret the cards.

Trust what comes to your mind as you keep each card placement's meaning in mind, look at the images and titles on the cards, or read through the guidebook descriptions and see certain words stand out to you. At that point, if you are still determining how a card you pulled correlates to the guide below, think of the opposite meaning of that card and see if that gives you more clarity. Listen to your inner knowing and what rings true to you.

Card 1 indicates the main thing that needs to be healed.

This may be something you lack, something you don't have confidence in, a trait or habit you may need to shift or release, or a belief you haven't fully adopted, etc.

Card 2 indicates what this thing is blocking you from.

This is where you are suffering, what you are struggling to do, or where you are getting stuck because of the unhealed issue from Card 1.

Card 3 indicates the lesson that can be learned.

This is the lesson, wisdom, trait, or opportunity that will be available to you through healing what you uncovered from Card 1.

THE PATH TO HEALING CARD SPREAD

Receive Guidance on How to Heal

If you ever find yourself aware of what you need to heal but uncertain how to begin healing it, use the card spread below for guidance on your next steps.

This card spread is designed specifically for use with The Wealthy Woman Oracle Deck but can be adapted for other decks.

Instructions:

1. Shuffle your deck while holding the following question in your mind: "How can I begin to heal this matter?"
2. Pull four cards, placing them in the provided configuration.
3. Use the guide below to interpret the cards.

Trust what comes to your mind as you keep each card placement's meaning in mind, look at the images and titles on the cards, or read through the guidebook descriptions and see certain words stand out to you. At that point, if you are still determining how a card you pulled correlates to the guide below, think of the opposite meaning of that card and see if that gives you more clarity. Listen to your inner knowing and what rings true to you.

Card 1 indicates what you can release.

This may be a habit, a fear, a story, a belief, or an energy that is preventing you from fully healing.

Card 2 indicates how you can release it.

Seek out modalities and practices that incorporate the essence of this card and allow you to release (or reduce) the essence of Card 1 from your life.

Card 3 indicates what you can embrace.

This may be a habit, a perspective, a narrative, a thought, or an energy that will help you to heal.

Card 4 indicates how you can embrace it.

Seek out modalities and practices that incorporate the essence of this card and allow you to bring more of the essence of Card 3 into your life.

"BY MENDING HOW YOU RELATE TO
MONEY, YOU RESTORE THE FLOW
OF IT IN YOUR LIFE."

When I think about money, my first thoughts are...

_____

_____

_____

_____

_____

_____

_____

When I talk about money, I use words that feel...

When I spend money, I feel...

One word that describes my current relationship with money is:

If I look at my relationship with money as though it were a relationship with another person, what would I say to money? Do I want to vent, complain, or express anything I'm dissatisfied with that money has or hasn't done in the past? I give myself permission to let it all out here. It's time money knows how I feel about it.

_____

_____

_____

_____

_____

_____

_____

_____

_____

_____

_____

_____

_____

_____

_____

_____

_____

_____

_____

_____

Continuing to look at my relationship with money as though money were a person, what would I like my relationship with money to look like from now on? What do I want from money? How do I want to feel around it? What do I want it to help me do?

_____

_____

_____

_____

_____

_____

_____

_____

_____

_____

_____

_____

_____

_____

_____

_____

_____

_____

_____

_____

_____

_____

If money were a person with whom I was trying to build a healthier, stronger, happier relationship, what would I take responsibility for so far in the relationship? What would I apologize for? What would I promise to do differently to play my part in improving this relationship?

_____

_____

_____

_____

_____

_____

_____

_____

_____

_____

_____

_____

_____

_____

_____

_____

_____

_____

_____

_____

_____

MONEY MANTRAS FOR HEALING YOUR RELATIONSHIP WITH MONEY

Choose one of the mantras below and repeat it 20 times. After doing so, reflect on what came up for you while reciting it.

My relationship with money grows stronger by the day.

I have the power to increase my wealth by strengthening my relationship with money.

The more love and respect I offer to my finances, the more they grow.

What were my experiences with this mantra? What thoughts, feelings, insights, or sensations did I experience?

_____

_____

_____

_____

_____

_____

_____

_____

_____

_____

_____

_____

_____

_____

_____

_____

_____

_____

_____

_____

_____

_____

"IT IS TIME FOR YOU TO BECOME YOUR OWN HEALER AND HEAL THROUGH LOVE."

Often, healing our money blocks is less about whatever wound or fear we have and instead is simply a by-product of restoring the flow of love within ourselves.

Use the following activation whenever you feel a lack of love for yourself or your relationship with money.

Close your eyes and take several deep, cleansing breaths.

Bring your attention to your body.

In your mind, ask, "Where in my body is the flow of love blocked?"

Pay attention to whatever area of your body you are first drawn to.

You may feel the block somewhere in your body, see it as a color or substance in your body, hear a part of your body named in your mind, or have an innate and inexplicable knowing.

Once you have identified the block's location, bring the energy of love to this area in your body.

See or feel the energy of love rushing to this area from all parts of yourself and dissolving this block.

Once the block is fully dissolved, visualize or feel the effortless flow of love energy through your body.

Allow it to flow, circulating and reaching every part of yourself.

Feel the love in you growing stronger, moving more swiftly and easily.

Take a few more deep breaths to strengthen this flow, and enjoy the feeling of it before opening your eyes.

What were my experiences with this activation? What thoughts, feelings, insights, or sensations did I experience?

_____

_____

_____

_____

_____

_____

_____

_____

_____

_____

_____

_____

_____

_____

_____

_____

_____

_____

_____

_____

_____

_____

_____

With the flow of love restored within me, what actions (big or small) do I feel inspired to take?

Looking at my answers to the previous question, the action I choose to take today is...

Today, I will bring more love to my money by...

"THE THING YOU PUT IN PLACE TO
PROTECT YOURSELF IS THE VERY THING
BLOCKING THE ABUNDANCE YOU SEEK."

In what ways do I try to protect myself when it comes to money?

_____

_____

_____

_____

_____

_____

_____

_____

_____

_____

_____

_____

_____

_____

_____

_____

_____

_____

_____

_____

_____

_____

_____

_____

When and why did I develop or adopt these defenses?

_____

_____

_____

_____

_____

_____

_____

_____

How do these defenses serve me and my finances?

_____

_____

_____

_____

_____

_____

_____

_____

_____

How do these defenses keep me and my finances stuck?

_____

_____

_____

_____

_____

_____

_____

_____

_____

_____

_____

_____

_____

_____

_____

_____

_____

_____

_____

_____

_____

_____

Money Mantras for Releasing Money Blocks

Choose one of the mantras below and repeat it 20 times. After doing so, reflect on what came up for you while reciting it.

I lovingly release whatever is blocking abundance.

I easily upgrade my beliefs and habits around money.

By releasing my old defenses, I make space for more prosperity.

What were my experiences with this mantra? What thoughts, feelings, insights, or sensations did I experience?

_____

_____

_____

_____

_____

_____

_____

_____

_____

_____

_____

_____

_____

_____

_____

_____

_____

_____

_____

_____

"TAP INTO THE DIVINE FLOW OF MONEY.
ALLOW IT TO FLOW TO YOU AND
THROUGH YOU."

Often, old money blocks are triggered whenever money flows in or out of our lives. Making peace with being a conduit for money helps us to detach from looking at money in terms of gains and losses but instead in terms of a continual flow.

Use the following activation whenever you feel resistance to money flowing in (receiving) or out (releasing) of your life.

As you breathe in, imagine a stream of prosperity flowing into your body and mentally say, "I receive money effortlessly for the highest good."

As you breathe out, imagine that stream flowing out. "I release money effortlessly for the highest good."

Complete at least five cycles of breathing in this way.

After the last breath, open your arms up to the sky and say the following statement to seal the energy of this practice: "I am a conduit for money, capable of receiving and giving in endless and limitless quantities."

What were my experiences with this activation? What thoughts, feelings, insights, or sensations did I experience?

_____

_____

_____

_____

_____

_____

_____

_____

_____

_____

_____

_____

_____

_____

_____

_____

_____

_____

_____

_____

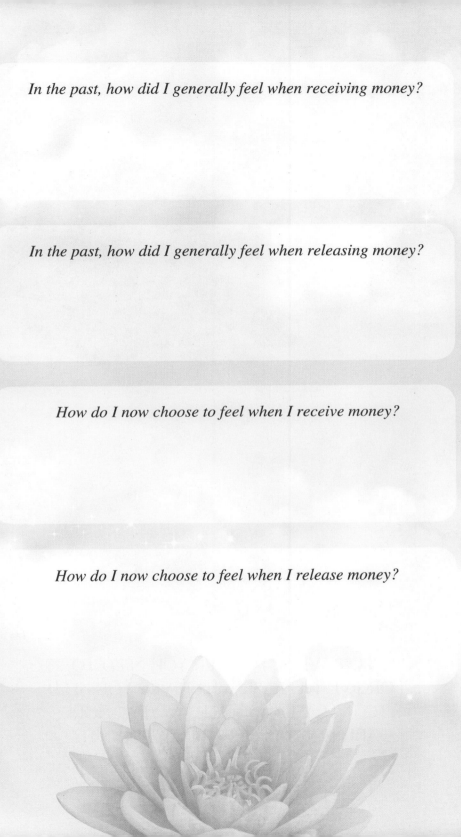

In the past, how did I generally feel when receiving money?

In the past, how did I generally feel when releasing money?

How do I now choose to feel when I receive money?

How do I now choose to feel when I release money?

"FORGIVE WHATEVER YOU NEED TO
FORGIVE. RELEASE WHATEVER YOU NEED
TO RELEASE. AND ALLOW NEW, MORE
ABUNDANT BELIEFS TO TAKE ROOT."

My energy around money feels the heaviest when...

My energy around money feels the lightest when...

Today, I will prioritize releasing the heaviness I feel around money by...

_____

_____

_____

_____

_____

_____

_____

_____

_____

_____

_____

_____

Today, I will prioritize increasing the lightness I feel around money by...

_____

_____

_____

_____

_____

_____

_____

What stories do I repeatedly tell myself about money?

How do these stories influence the actions I take when it comes to money?

_____

_____

_____

_____

_____

_____

_____

_____

_____

_____

_____

_____

_____

_____

_____

_____

_____

_____

_____

_____

"RELEASE WHAT IS NO LONGER SERVING
YOU AND ALLOW THE CHANGE TO
TRANSFORM YOU INTO A MORE ABUNDANT,
ALIGNED VERSION OF YOURSELF."

What is no longer serving me as I step into more abundance?

What am I now ready to release?

What would help me release this?

Who will I be once I release this?

Prayer for Healing

Whenever you find yourself clinging to what no longer serves you, say this prayer to release resistance to change and embrace your metamorphosis into a more abundant version of yourself. You can direct this prayer to a higher power, your higher self, your future self, or your spirit team.

I know that a more abundant version of myself is available, so I am requesting assistance to change.

Please give me the courage to release whatever no longer serves me.

Give me the strength to enter into the unknown of a new way of being.

Help me to release the fear of change so that I may see the beauty in it.

Remind me of the reward on the other side of this transformation.

Illuminate the path forward so that I may know how to gracefully release what needs to be released.

Bestow upon me the willpower and love I need to undergo this transformation.

I am ready and willing to be guided to change.

What were my experiences with this prayer? What thoughts, feelings, insights, or sensations did I experience?

Tuning into my inner guidance, what is the first step I am being called to take to release what will not serve me on my journey to abundance?

_____

_____

_____

_____

_____

_____

_____

_____

_____

_____

_____

_____

_____

_____

_____

_____

_____

_____

_____

_____

_____

TRUST

"Now is the time to find the answers that you're looking for—not by searching the world around you, but by looking deep within yourself."

There is no abundance without trust.

The Wealthy Woman knows that the trust she holds in herself is crucial to her ability to walk the path to prosperity.

For if she doubts her ability to create the money she desires...

If she forsakes her inner guidance...

If she puts her faith in fear instead of in her vision...

She will be led astray from the abundance she seeks.

The Wealthy Woman knows that the road to wealth has many twists and turns—far too many for her to foresee or predict. She journeys forward intentionally, taking care to look within so that she may determine which turn to take or which detours to make. She seeks every opportunity to connect more with herself and strengthen her belief that she is her own best guide.

Above all, the Wealthy Woman constantly reminds herself of her power so that she can journey boldly into the unknown, unafraid of what she might find or what challenges she might meet on her way to wild abundance. A smile plays on her lips and a surge of power flows through her as she reminds herself of what she knows to be true: *When I am rich in trust, no riches are off-limits to me.*

Trusting the Path to Prosperity

Reaching new levels of wealth will require you to think,

act, and be different from how you have ever been. It requires a venture into the unknown and many, many ego deaths. Any change, big or small, means that some part of your identity must die to make space for a new —more abundant—version of yourself to be born.

As you take bold actions and move outside your comfort zone on your path to abundance, you may discover that you're questioning yourself more than ever before. You may feel uncertain of what the future holds, fearful of what may (or may not) come to be, and wonder whether it would be better not to pursue the prosperity your soul is yearning for. This is where trust is essential.

The following pages contain questions, mantras, and exercises to help you forge a strong sense of self-trust and universal trust. These two forms of trust will guide you through the uncertainties and challenges that will spring up as you venture toward the financial reality you desire.

Self-trust allows you to hear and act more clearly on your inner guidance. It's the constant whisper of "I can do this" in the back of your mind. It's the unshakeable belief that you can handle anything that comes your way.

Universal trust allows you to release what you cannot control and put your faith in a higher power or energy. It's your connection and co-creation with the universe. It's the willingness to allow yourself to be supported, guided, or even redirected to your desires.

Without trust in yourself, you will never be willing to

become a different version of yourself—because that's the most terrifying thing to your ego. Without trust in something greater than you—be it a universal power, a divine energy, your soul, or the limitless possibility of the infinite universe we exist in—you will never be willing to take great leaps toward your desires.

Trust is what grants us the ability to take bold actions that move us closer into alignment with the most abundant version of ourselves. Especially when the actions we feel called to take appear to be unrelated to money. Often, the most inconsequential and illogical actions end up being the ones that take us exactly where we want to go.

The fastest way to create trust is by experimenting with it and showing your logical mind evidence that it's safe to trust in yourself or something bigger than you. As you build deeper levels of trust, notice the sacred bond you are forming with yourself and the strength you can draw upon from the world around you. This bond is a form of abundance in itself. As it takes root within you, it changes your way of moving through the world, making material abundance more and more inevitable in your life.

CARD SPREADS

Strengthening Self-Trust Card Spread

How You Can Trust Yourself More Fully

Should you ever question your ability to create the wealth you desire or waver in your belief that it is safe to trust your inner guidance, use the following card spread to receive guidance on how you can most powerfully strengthen your trust in yourself.

This card spread is designed specifically for use with The Wealthy Woman Oracle Deck but can be adapted for other decks.

Instructions:

1. Shuffle your deck while holding the following question in your mind: "How can I strengthen my trust in myself?"
2. Pull three cards, placing them in the provided configuration.
3. Use the guide below to interpret the cards.

Trust what comes to your mind as you keep each card placement's meaning in mind, look at the images and titles on the cards, or read through the guidebook descriptions and see certain words stand out to you. At that point, if you are still determining how a card you pulled correlates to the guide below, think of the opposite meaning of that card and see if that gives you more clarity. Listen to your inner knowing and what rings true to you.

Card 1 indicates where you are not fully trusting yourself. This is where you want to focus on strengthening your trust in yourself so that you can embody or allow more security within yourself in this area.

Card 2 indicates how to strengthen this area of trust.

This is how you can begin to build more trust in the area indicated by Card 1. This could be an energy to embody, an action to take, or something to focus on.

Card 3 indicates what you stand to gain from strengthening your trust in this area.

This is what wisdom, blessing, soul gift, or opportunity will be available to you once you strengthen the area indicated by Card 1.

Universal Unity Card Spread

How You Can More Deeply Trust Something Greater Than Yourself

If you struggle to trust in your higher self, a higher power, or any other force greater than yourself, use this spread to uncover how you can cultivate deeper universal trust.

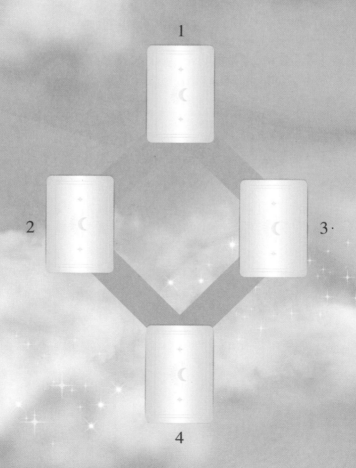

This card spread is designed specifically for use with The Wealthy Woman Oracle Deck but can be adapted for other decks.

Instructions:

1. Shuffle your deck while holding the following question in your mind: "How can I strengthen my universal trust?"
2. Pull four cards, placing them in the provided configuration.
3. Use the guide below to interpret the cards.

Trust what comes to your mind as you keep each card placement's meaning in mind, look at the images and titles on the cards, or read through the guidebook descriptions and see certain words stand out to you. At that point, if you are still determining how a card you pulled correlates to the guide below, think of the opposite meaning of that card and see if that gives you more clarity. Listen to your inner knowing and what rings true to you.

◆

Card 1 indicates what you are being asked to trust.

This is where the universe (or some greater force) wants to support you more fully and asks you to be receptive.

Card 2 indicates how you can build up that trust.

This could be an energy to embody, an action to take, or something to focus on that will allow you to open yourself up to receiving the universal support offered to you per Card 1.

Card 3 indicates why it may feel difficult for you to trust in this way.

This may be a block, a story, or a habit keeping you from feeling comfortable receiving support per Card 1.

Card 4 indicates a promise from the universe.

This is what wisdom, blessing, soul gift, or opportunity will be available to you once you trust more in the support offered by Card 1.

"TRUST YOUR OWN INTERNAL
GUIDANCE TO LEAD YOU TO THE
WEALTH YOU DESIRE."

My inner guidance sounds or feels like...

My inner guidance is the strongest in this part of my body...

My inner guidance is the strongest in situations concerning...

When I think about money, my inner guidance...

_____

_____

_____

_____

_____

_____

_____

_____

On a scale from 1 to 10, I rate my current willingness to rely on my inner guidance to make decisions around money as...

What are all the times I can recall that I acted on my inner guidance
around money matters in the past?

_____

_____

_____

_____

_____

_____

_____

_____

_____

_____

_____

_____

_____

_____

_____

_____

_____

_____

_____

_____

_____

_____

How did I feel when acting on that inner guidance in each of those instances? How did each of those instances play out?

_____

_____

_____

_____

_____

_____

_____

_____

_____

_____

_____

_____

_____

_____

_____

_____

_____

_____

_____

_____

_____

_____

What are all the times I can recall that I acted against my inner guidance
around money matters in the past?

_____

_____

_____

_____

_____

_____

_____

_____

_____

_____

_____

_____

_____

_____

_____

_____

_____

_____

_____

_____

_____

How did I feel when I ignored my inner guidance in each instance? How did each of those instances play out?

_____

_____

_____

_____

_____

_____

_____

_____

_____

_____

_____

_____

_____

_____

_____

_____

_____

_____

_____

_____

_____

_____

Based on the times I have or haven't trusted my inner guidance, what stories or beliefs have I created within myself around trusting my inner guidance about money matters?

_____

_____

_____

_____

_____

_____

_____

_____

_____

_____

_____

_____

_____

_____

_____

_____

_____

_____

_____

_____

_____

Money Mantras for Cultivating Self-Trust

Choose one of the mantras below and repeat it 20 times. After doing so, reflect on what came up for you while reciting it.

My inner guidance is always guiding me to the abundance I seek.

It is safe to trust my inner guidance in money matters.

I am my own best guide on the path to prosperity.

What were my experiences with this mantra? What thoughts, feelings, insights, or sensations did I experience?

"YOU, AND YOU ALONE, HOLD THE KEY TO
YOUR OWN ABUNDANCE."

In order to hear our inner guidance, we must make space for it to speak—and we must listen. Use the following activation whenever you have difficulty hearing your inner guidance (especially around money).

Note: you can adjust the question you ask in the activation to be more geared toward abundance or a specific financial situation, but the answers we seek often do not appear to be connected to money at first glance. This is why using a general question can unlock more guidance from within ourselves. Our inner guidance often gives us the next step that will lead us, directly or indirectly, to the wealth we desire. Do not judge what comes up; just listen.

———————————

Sit in a quiet area.

Close your eyes and take a few breaths to center yourself in the present moment.

Envision yourself sitting in a sacred location—perhaps a building or location in nature that feels serene to you.

Feel a wave of safety and calm wash over you as you notice your inner guidance sitting next to you.

Take note of what form your inner guidance takes. What does it look like? Is it a person, an animal, a sphere of light, or something else?

Greet your inner guidance and ask, "What do you want me to know?"

Wait and listen to what your inner guidance has to say. Take note if you feel any sensations in your body as your inner guidance shares whatever wisdom it has with you.

Thank your inner guidance for whatever it shared with you.

If your inner guidance didn't share anything, thank it for its presence and try to connect with it again later. (Sometimes there isn't any guidance we need to hear at the moment, or we need to become more practiced to properly hear the guidance that is trying to come through.)

Take another deep breath and bring your awareness back to the present moment, then open your eyes.

What were my experiences with this activation? What thoughts, feelings, insights, or sensations did I experience?

_____

_____

_____

_____

_____

_____

_____

_____

_____

_____

_____

_____

_____

_____

_____

_____

_____

_____

_____

_____

_____

_____

The guidance I received feels...

Do I want to act on this guidance?

If I want to act on this guidance, what is one thing I can do to commit to honoring it?

If I do not want to act on this guidance, why is that? Am I choosing not to act from a more accurate form of inner guidance or from fear?

"TRUST THAT THE FASTEST WAY TO
MANIFEST MORE MONEY INTO YOUR
EXPERIENCE IS BY FOLLOWING
WHAT EXCITES YOU."

Today, I am most excited to...

_____

_____

_____

_____

The thing that feels best to me to do right now is...

_____

_____

_____

_____

*Doing these things could potentially lead me to more
abundance because...*

_____

_____

_____

_____

*How can I honor these things that feel exciting or good
to me today, even if only in a small way?*

After acting on my answers to the previous questions, how did things go? Did anything positive happen when I acted on what excited or felt good to me? Did it lead me somewhere unexpected?

_____

_____

_____

_____

_____

_____

_____

_____

_____

_____

_____

_____

_____

_____

_____

_____

_____

_____

_____

_____

Money Mantras for Cultivating Universal Trust

Choose one of the mantras below and repeat it 20 times. After doing so, reflect on what came up for you while reciting it.

The universe is always working to bring me the abundance I desire.

I do not have to walk the path to prosperity alone.

I am divinely supported and always guided to more abundance.

What were my experiences with this mantra? What thoughts, feelings, insights, or sensations did I experience?

_____
_____
_____
_____
_____
_____
_____
_____
_____
_____
_____
_____
_____
_____
_____
_____
_____
_____
_____
_____
_____
_____

"UNBURDEN YOURSELF FROM THE
IMPOSSIBLE TASK OF CONTROLLING
WHAT YOU CANNOT."

When we try to control things that we can't control (like whether someone decides to hire us, pay us, gift us money, etc.), we create blocks between ourselves and the money we desire.

It is important to remember to focus on what you can control and offer anything you cannot control to the universe, trusting it will take care of it for you in whatever way serves your highest good. In doing this, you free up more of your mental and physical energy to apply to the things you can control— allowing you to move more swiftly and clearly toward prosperity.

Use the following activation whenever you want to surrender something you cannot control around money and entrust the universe to take care of it for you.

———————————

Cup your hands out in front of you with your palms up to the sky.

Feel all the energy, worries, and thoughts of the things you cannot control pouring from your heart, head, or wherever they are stored and into your hands.

Raise your hands up to the sky and ask the universe to take this all from you:

"I cannot hold this, and I know I am not meant to. Please take this from me and tend to it for my highest good and the highest good of those around me.

I release control and trust that you will take care of this in whatever way will help guide me toward more love and abundance.

Thank you, thank you, thank you."

Feel the weight of these burdens lift from your hands as the universe takes them from you.

Take a few moments to feel the lightness and space within your body now that these burdens are no longer stored there.

Seal the practice with a deep breath of gratitude for the universe and your willingness to surrender.

What were my experiences with this activation? What thoughts, feelings, insights, or sensations did I experience?

_____

_____

_____

_____

_____

_____

_____

_____

_____

_____

_____

_____

_____

_____

_____

_____

_____

_____

_____

_____

_____

Now that I have surrendered what I cannot control around money, I feel inspired to...

What is the most magical way I can imagine the universe tending to what I have surrendered? What would be a miraculous outcome?

No matter what happens with these things I've surrendered, I choose to trust that the universe...

"BECOME A STUDENT AND ALLOW THE
UNIVERSE TO HELP YOU GROW INTO
GREATER PROSPERITY."

Some positive things I am experiencing around money right now are...

Some negative things I am experiencing around money right now are...

*How could these things be happening **for** me?*

What lessons might the universe offer me through whatever I am currently experiencing around money?

_____

_____

_____

_____

_____

_____

_____

_____

_____

_____

_____

_____

_____

_____

_____

_____

_____

_____

_____

_____

_____

_____

_____

_____

Can I imagine a situation in the future where I may look back at this moment with gratitude for what it catapulted me towards? What does that future situation look like?

_____

_____

_____

_____

_____

_____

_____

_____

_____

_____

_____

_____

_____

_____

_____

_____

_____

_____

_____

"PROSPERITY IN ALL FORMS IS JUST
WAITING FOR YOU TO CLAIM IT."

What action do I intuitively know I need to take to bring more abundance into my life?

As I take this action, I will choose to trust the universe to...

It is safe to trust that I can figure out whatever happens after taking this action because...

Prayer for Trust

Following our inner guidance and guidance from the universe can often feel intimidating as we are pushed out of our comfort zone. But if you do not change, neither will your financial reality. You will stay stagnant on the path to prosperity. You must dig deep into the trust you have cultivated within yourself and the universe to find the courage to leap into the unknown. Use the prayer below whenever you want to lean on this sacred trust to move toward abundance.

I know that in every moment, I have a choice.

A choice to put my trust in my inner guidance…

Or a choice to put my trust in my fear.

Today, I choose to put my trust in that which excites me, inspires me, feels good to me, and feels right to me.

Today, I choose not to bow to any worries of what might be or the expectations of others.

Instead, I choose to leap into what is aligned for me—even if I do not know where I will land.

I call on the forces of the universe to see that I am delivered safely to wherever I need to be.

I call on my inner guidance to help me navigate whatever terrain I may find myself upon, knowing that I can always figure out the next right step and then the next until I arrive at the abundance I seek.

I put my trust in the universe, and I put my trust in myself.

When I am rich in trust, no riches are off-limits to me.

What were my experiences with this prayer? What thoughts, feelings, insights, or sensations did I experience?

_____

_____

_____

_____

_____

_____

_____

_____

_____

_____

_____

_____

_____

_____

_____

_____

_____

_____

_____

_____

Tuning to my inner guidance, what first step must I now take to leap toward the abundance I want?

_____

_____

_____

_____

_____

_____

_____

What do I choose to entrust to the universe as I take this step?

_____

_____

_____

_____

_____

_____

_____

_____

_____

WORTHINESS

"It is your destiny to wholeheartedly embrace the greatness within you. When you do so, abundance in all forms—riches, adoration, influence—will be magnetized to you."

There is no question in the Wealthy Woman's mind that she is deserving or capable of having the wealth she desires. She does not measure her worth or potential based on the level of worldly prosperity she currently possesses—or on how much she is willing to struggle or sacrifice. She knows that she is already infinitely wealthy within—and that the acquisition of outward, material abundance is merely a matter of allowing the wealth of her soul to shine through.

The Wealthy Woman walks the path to abundance with a confident, unhurried stride. As she does, she does not seek out abundance. Rather, she looks for opportunities to better understand and share her unique gifts with the world. Within her is the deep knowing that these innate qualities she possesses are what make her valuable beyond measure—and will easily bring abundance to her.

It is from this place of deep understanding of her innate worth that the Wealthy Woman can selflessly offer her gifts to those who need them and, in return, gracefully receive all the prosperous blessings that the universe bestows upon her.

Walking in Worthiness

The key to an overflow of abundance does not lie in struggling. In fact, hard work for the sake of hard work often impedes the flow of prosperity. The truth is that you are naturally abundant. You are part of this infinite, expansive universe—existing amongst the stars and all manner of wonders.

It is only when you understand how wondrous *you* are —when you tap into the innate abundance of your soul —that wealth becomes inevitable in your life.

But how do you understand the immeasurable value that you possess?

How do you translate the intangible wealth you hold within you into material abundance?

The answer is simple: understand and share your unique gifts.

Your keys to abundance are the things that come easily to you, excite you, and make you feel alive. For what comes easily to you does not come easily to everyone. What interests you, what intrigues you, and what inspires you is unique to you. These traits and interests are your unique gifts. They're meant to be shared with the world and bring abundance into your life.

Your gifts hold so much value to yourself and others. When leveraged freely and intentionally, these gifts allow money to flow to you in a natural, easy, and fulfilling way. When you know the full value of your gifts, any guilt or hesitation around receiving money is eradicated, for you know that you are divinely worthy of abundance and that your wealth benefits everyone.

It is far too easy to take your gifts for granted and sometimes even be completely unaware of them within yourself. When you live your whole life as you, it's hard to gain perspective on what makes you unique.

This section contains questions, mantras, and exercises to help you identify, value, and leverage your unique gifts for abundance and cultivate an overall understanding of your innate worthiness. You have countless gifts, so revisit these concepts regularly to uncover more of your gifts and increase your capacity for creating abundance over time.

If your mind (or other people) tries to convince you that financial wealth cannot be so easy, remember that hard work is not the secret to money. The secret is knowing your worth and using your gifts to their fullest potential. The only hard work necessary for wealth is the effort it takes to remember the value of your gifts in a world that has told you they're not valuable.

Your gifts are meant to make you rich. When you share your gifts, you enrich the world in a way that only you can. This offering of your most sacred self to the world unfurls the path to prosperity before you, leading you to abundance beyond your wildest dreams.

CARD ✦ SPREADS

SOUL GIFT DISCOVERY CARD SPREAD

Uncover and Understand the Value of Your Soul Gifts

Whenever you feel called to discover a gift that you have and learn to see its value (so that you may use it to call in more abundance), use the following card spread to gain clarity on whatever gift you are ready to uncover within yourself.

This card spread is designed specifically for use with The Wealthy Woman Oracle Deck but can be adapted for other decks.

Instructions:

1. Shuffle your deck while holding the following question in your mind: "What gift do I possess that is ready to be uncovered or better understood?"
2. Pull five cards, placing them in the provided configuration.
3. Use the guide below to interpret the cards.

Trust what comes to your mind as you keep each card placement's meaning in mind, look at the images and titles on the cards, or read through the guidebook descriptions and see certain words stand out to you. At that point, if you are still determining how a card you pulled correlates to the guide below, think of the opposite meaning of that card and see if that gives you more clarity. Listen to your inner knowing and what rings true to you.

Card 1 indicates what gift is ready to be uncovered.
This may be a skill or trait that comes easily to you, an energy you naturally carry, a habit you have, a way you help others, or an area in which you are particularly skilled or interested.

Card 2 indicates what is keeping you from fully understanding the value of this gift.
This is a habit, block, lack of something, story, or pattern that is preventing you from fully understanding how valuable the gift from Card 1 is.

Card 3 indicates what you can do to see the value of this gift more clearly.
This could be an area to heal, an energy to embody, a practice to cultivate, or a mentality to adopt that will help you deepen your understanding of the value of the gift revealed by Card 1.

Card 4 indicates how this gift can be used to help you create more wealth in your life.
This may be how the gift from Card 1 can be shared with others, how it can help you heal money blocks, how it can help you deepen your sense of worthiness, or how you can apply it to money-making activities or your finances.

Card 5 indicates the full power of this gift.
This may be how others see the gift from Card 1 in you, the potential impact it may have in your life, or how it may change others' lives for the better.

Soul Riches Card Spread

How to Be Compensated for Your Soul Gift

Once you have identified a soul gift (of which you have many) and seen its value, use the following card spread to receive guidance on how you can best leverage this gift to create more abundance in your life.

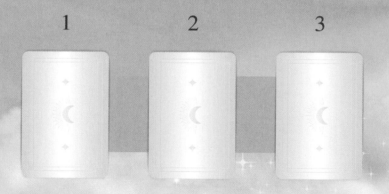

This card spread is designed specifically for use with The Wealthy Woman Oracle Deck but can be adapted for other decks.

Instructions:

1. Shuffle your deck while holding the gift you've identified, plus the following question in your mind: "How can this gift be used to create more abundance in my life?"
2. Pull three cards, placing them in the provided configuration.
3. Use the guide below to interpret the cards.

Trust what comes to your mind as you keep each card placement's meaning in mind, look at the images and titles on the cards, or read through the guidebook descriptions and see certain words stand out to you. At that point, if you are still determining how a card you pulled correlates to the guide below, think of the opposite meaning of that card and see if that gives you more clarity. Listen to your inner knowing and what rings true to you.

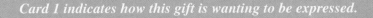

Card 1 indicates how this gift is wanting to be expressed.

This may be about how you can share it with others, what area of your life it will be most useful in, or a habit or skill that would be beneficial to amplify its value.

Card 2 indicates how this gift can be used for the highest good.

This could be how using this gift can benefit others or how it can improve your relationship with others.

Card 3 indicates how this gift can be used to call more financial abundance into your life.

This may be how you can create a product or service from this gift, how you can incorporate this gift into your work or money-related activities, or other steps you can take to leverage this gift for wealth in an aligned way.

"THERE IS NOTHING YOU NEED TO DO OR BECOME
IN ORDER TO BE WORTHY OF YOUR DESIRES.

YOU ARE ALREADY DESERVING.

ALL THAT IS REQUESTED IS THAT YOU
ACKNOWLEDGE THIS INNATE VALUE AND
WORTHINESS THAT YOU ALREADY POSSESS."

I feel most like myself when...

I am most inspired when...

I am most confident when...

I am at my best when...

What comes easily to me? Digging deep into myself, what soft skills, hard skills, or qualities do I possess?

_____

_____

_____

_____

_____

_____

_____

_____

_____

_____

_____

_____

_____

_____

_____

_____

_____

_____

_____

_____

_____

Which of the things from my previous answer do I feel are my biggest gifts and why?

_____

_____

_____

_____

_____

_____

_____

_____

Why are each of my notable gifts valuable to me?

_____

_____

_____

_____

_____

_____

_____

_____

What are some ways I can more deeply and intentionally integrate my notable gifts into my work, career, or finances?

_____

_____

_____

_____

_____

_____

_____

_____

_____

_____

_____

_____

_____

_____

_____

_____

_____

_____

_____

_____

_____

_____

MONEY MANTRAS FOR EMBRACING YOUR GIFTS

Choose one of the mantras below and repeat it 20 times. After doing so, reflect on what came up for you while reciting it.

The things that come easily to me do not come easily to everyone else.

The things that come easily to me are worthy of massive compensation.

The things that come easily to me are my greatest gifts for making money.

What were my experiences with this mantra? What thoughts, feelings, insights, or sensations did I experience?

_____

_____

_____

_____

_____

_____

_____

_____

_____

_____

_____

_____

_____

_____

_____

_____

_____

_____

_____

_____

_____

"CULTIVATE YOUR INNER GARDEN
OF WEALTH BY REVELING IN
YOUR SOUL'S GIFTS."

Soul Gift Activation

We must first understand our gifts in order to share them with the world and unlock an effortless flow of abundance.

Use the following activation to identify, activate, or amplify the immense value of any of your gifts. This can be particularly useful when intentionally applying a gift to create more abundance in your life for the first time or when you feel disconnected from the value of your gifts.

Take a deep breath and bring your attention to your body.

Visualize or sense dozens (or even hundreds) of tiny spheres of light joyfully bobbing and floating within you—these are your soul gifts.

Ask the universe to show you the specific gift you wish to activate (or ask it to show you which gift would serve you most to activate right now).

Focus your attention on whichever sphere of light stands out to you.

Breathe into this sphere. With each inhale and exhale, feel the sphere—your gift—grow brighter and bigger, filling your body with its light.

Allow this light to radiate outward from you, extending beyond your body to bless everything and everyone around you.

As you share this light with the world, feel the universe's gratitude for your willingness to share this gift.

Sense the energy of abundance begin to trickle into your body and grow the light of your gift even brighter. The brighter this light glows, the more the energy of abundance pours into you as compensation from the universe for your gifts.

Continue to breathe and feel your gift's light grow and the energy of abundance increase within you for as long as it feels good to you.

Then, place your hands over your heart and thank yourself for sharing this light with the world.

Go about your day knowing this gift is now activated within you, and look for opportunities to share it.

What were my experiences with this activation? What thoughts, feelings, insights, or sensations did I experience?

_____

_____

_____

_____

_____

_____

_____

_____

_____

_____

_____

_____

_____

_____

_____

_____

_____

_____

_____

_____

_____

_____

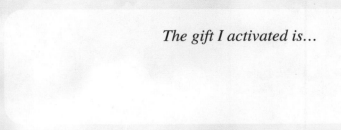

The gift I activated is...

This gift is immensely valuable because...

I am worthy of being financially compensated for this gift because...

What is one way I can use this gift in my money-related activities today?

"YOU ARE BEING CALLED TO
RETURN TO THE WEALTH THAT IS
CARRIED WITHIN YOUR SOUL."

When I think about how worthy I am of creating the wealth I desire in my life, I feel...

_____

_____

_____

_____

I feel the most worthy of creating the wealth I desire when...

_____

_____

_____

_____

When I think about how capable I am of creating the wealth I desire in my life, I feel...

_____

_____

_____

_____

I feel the most capable of creating the wealth I desire when...

_____

_____

_____

_____

Money Mantras for Wealth Creation

Choose one of the mantras below and repeat it 20 times. After doing so, reflect on what came up for you while reciting it.

I am capable of creating more wealth than I have ever imagined.

Making money comes easily and naturally to me.

I am uniquely and innately valuable.

What were my experiences with this mantra? What thoughts, feelings, insights, or sensations did I experience?

_____
_____
_____
_____
_____
_____
_____
_____
_____
_____
_____
_____
_____
_____
_____
_____
_____
_____
_____
_____
_____

"MONEY AND WEALTH DO NOT DISCRIMINATE
BASED ON HOW MUCH YOU WORK OR HOW
HARD YOU FORGE AHEAD.

IN FACT, ABUNDANCE CAN MORE EASILY COME
TO YOU WHEN YOU AREN'T ALWAYS MOVING."

ABUNDANCE IN STILLNESS ACTIVATION

By owning your innate worthiness for wealth and your uniquely valuable gifts, you open yourself up to receiving abundance with increasing ease. The truth is that money—and all forms of abundance—are often trying to flow to us. But as much as we say we want effortless wealth, we rarely feel worthy or capable of it. This results in us working so much harder than we need to in order to try to finally achieve that feeling of being or doing enough to have the prosperity we want.

When working harder than necessary, we often move so quickly that we miss countless opportunities for abundance to come to us easily. Sometimes, all we need to do is slow down and allow the money to catch up with us.

Use the following activation whenever you want to open yourself up to receive with more ease and less struggle.

———————

Close your eyes and bring your attention inward.

Envision yourself sitting by a stream of water.

This stream represents the current flow of abundance in your life.

As you sit and observe the stream, notice how it grows swifter and broader.

Feel the energy of abundance swell within you as the stream increases in strength. Notice that in order for the stream of abundance to flow more fluidly, all you must do is sit and allow it to increase.

But if you should try to meddle with the stream by placing rocks or your hands in it—you only impede its flow.

Sit and observe this stream for as long as it feels good to do so, seeing it grow stronger and feeling the sensation of abundance within you increase.

As you do, start to notice how different things drift to you down the stream—perhaps you see money, opportunities, or gifts from nature floating on the water's surface.

Gently take each of these blessings from the stream as they float in front of you.

When you are ready to close out this practice, take a deep breath and thank the stream for all it has delivered to you.

As you open your eyes, remember that this stillness is all that is required of you to increase the flow of abundance. Your awareness and willingness are all that are required of you to act on the abundance that is carried your way.

What were my experiences with this activation? What thoughts, feelings, insights, or sensations did I experience?

Now that I have taken a moment to be still, I feel inspired to...

_____

_____

_____

_____

_____

_____

_____

_____

_____

_____

_____

_____

What is the most magical way I can imagine abundance coming to me?

_____

_____

_____

_____

_____

_____

_____

"WHEN YOU ACCEPT
ABUNDANCE WITHOUT QUESTION,
THE JOY YOU FEEL IS ECHOED IN
THE PLEASURE OF THE PERSON
WHO GAVE IT TO YOU."

When people give me gifts or money, I feel…

When I allow others to give me gifts or money, others benefit because…

I love to receive…

The more abundance I receive, the more I…

*What times have I deflected—or not been open to gracefully
and effortlessly receiving—money, gifts, compliments,
assistance, or other forms of abundance?*

_____

_____

_____

_____

_____

_____

_____

_____

_____

_____

_____

_____

_____

_____

_____

_____

_____

_____

_____

_____

_____

How did I feel in those instances?

_____

_____

_____

_____

_____

_____

_____

◆ ◆ ◆

How do I think others felt in those instances?

_____

_____

_____

_____

_____

_____

_____

_____

Why does it benefit me to be more open to receive from others?

_____

_____

_____

_____

_____

_____

_____

Why does it benefit others when they can give to me?

"THE MORE YOU USE MONEY
WITH THE INTENT TO ALWAYS
DO THE HIGHEST GOOD IN THE
WORLD, THE MORE MONEY FINDS
ITS WAY BACK TO YOU."

Being wealthy allows me to…

By having financial abundance, I am a better person because…

When I am financially abundant, others benefit because…

Prayer for Worthiness

The more wealth we have, the more good we can do in the world. Yet, we often forget how money can be a force for love and positive change—and instead, we slip into feeling selfish, greedy, or wholly unworthy of the abundance we desire (or even have). Remembering that our ability to help others only increases as our prosperity increases allows us to stay connected to our innate worthiness and receive (and use) money more easily.
Use the prayer below whenever you want to reconnect with your innate worthiness and capacity for good regarding wealth.

I am opening my heart and soul up to receive.

I anchor into my worthiness and the value I carry.

I hold my gifts in the highest esteem and deepest gratitude.

I open myself to an effortless flow of abundance beyond my wildest dreams.

Please, universe, help me to remember my sacred worth.

Help me know how to best use the wealth I currently possess—and all wealth that flows to me—for the highest good, for I wish to help myself to thrive.

And I wish to help others to live in abundance, as well.

I now allow my abundance to grow with ease so that I may be a light for all.

What were my experiences with this prayer? What thoughts, feelings, insights, or sensations did I experience?

_____

_____

_____

_____

_____

_____

_____

_____

_____

_____

_____

_____

_____

_____

_____

_____

_____

_____

_____

_____

_____

_____

_____

_____

_____

Tuning into my heart, what do I know to be true about my gifts,
innate value, and worthiness of abundance?

_____

_____

_____

_____

_____

_____

_____

_____

What is one thing I can do today with whatever abundance I
have available to me right now (my gifts, energy, money, etc.)
that can help others and myself thrive?

VISION

"You are not at the whim of the universe.
*You **are** the universe. And through your*
actions all wealth flows."

As the Wealthy Woman walks the path to prosperity, she is truly walking two paths: the physical path that will eventually lead her to the material abundance she desires and the inner path that allows her instantaneous access to true wealth. While she knows that the physical path requires care and attention, she also knows that the inner path is the one that will ultimately deliver her to all prosperity, inside and outside. For the inner path is what shapes the outer path.

The Wealthy Woman's inner journey into the depths of her healing, trust, and worthiness allows her to walk the outer path more confidently. Her inner journey to fully hold and embody the energy of abundance enables her to stay on the outer path without faltering. So, as she journeys forth in the material world, the Wealthy Woman prioritizes her inner world, holding the vision of the wealth she desires in her mind so that she may navigate to it without distraction. With this vision of abundance solidified in her mind, she can easily access the energy of it—the joy, the fulfillment, the security, the freedom, the wealth—and revel in it.

Her every step on the outer path to prosperity radiates the energy of her inner wealth, thus drawing it closer to her and smoothing the physical path before her. When she does arrive at the material abundance she seeks, she realizes that she did not journey to it but created it—a physical manifestation of the Wealthy Woman she has awakened within herself.

The road to the wealth you desire will be infinitely easier to travel when you can firmly hold the vision of your desired prosperity in your mind and heart. Often, along the way to abundance, we tend to look around and doubt if we'll ever get there. The truth is that we don't know *how* we'll get to the abundance we desire. We don't know what the path will look like or where it will twist and turn. This truth is why it is so important to do the healing, trust, and worthiness work we've covered so far… but this is also why it is important to embody the wealth you desire on an energetic and mental level before you receive it on the physical level. After all, it's easy to look at where you are and focus on the lack of what you desire at this moment. But when you focus solely on what you do not have right now, you are closing yourself off to the possibility that this moment holds to move you closer to what you do want.

The great work of walking the path to wealth is not in the journey itself but in your willingness and ability to *become* the wealth you desire. The following pages contain questions, mantras, and exercises to help you identify and hold the vision of the wealth you desire.

It may take time for you to be able to comfortably hold the vision and energy of your next level of abundance— especially if you have spent years (or most of your life) focusing on the vision and energy of *not* having it. Continue to remind yourself of the power you hold in each moment to reconnect with the vision of your wealth.

You do not need to wait for the wealth you desire to arrive in physical form before you feel abundant. You are so powerful that you can conjure up those feelings now —and at any moment. In fact, feeling as though you already possess that prosperity and reveling in that inner experience will draw you closer to its physical realization.

Allow your vision to transform you. Allow yourself to feel the joy, security, freedom, and overall energy of abundance so that you radiate it out into the world.

Allow yourself to live more and more in the inner reality of the wealth you desire before it shows up. This willingness to experience the sensations and thoughts of wealth before it arrives in your life is how you fully activate the Wealthy Woman within you. This is how you become her. This is the true Way of the Wealthy Woman.

CARD SPREADS

WEALTH CONNECTION
CARD SPREAD

Reconnect With Your Vision of Wealth

Should you find yourself getting caught up in where you currently are (and the lack of the abundance you desire), use the following card spread to uncover how you can most easily reconnect with the vision of the wealth you desire.

This card spread is designed specifically for use with The Wealthy Woman Oracle Deck but can be adapted for other decks.

Instructions:

1. Shuffle your deck while holding the gift you've identified, plus the following question in your mind: "How can I reconnect with the vision of my desired wealth?"
2. Pull three cards, placing them in the provided configuration.
3. Use the guide below to interpret the cards.

Trust what comes to your mind as you keep each card placement's meaning in mind, look at the images and titles on the cards, or read through the guidebook descriptions and see certain words stand out to you. At that point, if you are still determining how a card you pulled correlates to the guide below, think of the opposite meaning of that card and see if that gives you more clarity. Listen to your inner knowing and what rings true to you.

◆

Card 1 indicates how to detach from what is.

This may be an energy to embody, a new perspective to adopt, or a practice to do to detach from any sense of lack in the present moment.

Card 2 indicates how to realign with your vision of wealth.

This could be something to focus on at this moment, a practice to do, or something to incorporate into your life to help you connect with your vision of what your life will look and feel like once you've received the wealth you desire.

Card 3 indicates how to feel abundant now.

This may be a mindset to shift into, an action to take, or something to reflect on that will allow you to feel as though you already have all the wealth you desire now (before it physically manifests).

Abundance Amplification Card Spread

Hold the Vision and Energy of Your Desired Wealth

Whenever you feel called to deepen your ability to hold and embody the vision of your desired wealth, use the following card spread to receive guidance to help you amplify the energy of abundance within yourself.

This card spread is designed specifically for use with The Wealthy Woman Oracle Deck but can be adapted for other decks.

Instructions:

1. Shuffle your deck while holding the gift you've identified, plus the following question in your mind: "How can I more powerfully hold and embody my vision of the wealth I desire?"
2. Pull five cards, placing them in the provided configuration.
3. Use the guide below to interpret the cards.

Trust what comes to your mind as you keep each card placement's meaning in mind, look at the images and titles on the cards, or read through the guidebook descriptions and see certain words stand out to you. At that point, if you are still determining how a card you pulled correlates to the guide below, think of the opposite meaning of that card and see if that gives you more clarity. Listen to your inner knowing and what rings true to you.

Card 1 indicates how your current situation is happening for you.

This offers a new perspective, insight, or lesson that is being offered to you where you are right now that will help you on your path to the abundance you desire.

Card 2 indicates what to focus on to hold the vision.

This could be what you can focus on, a habit you can cultivate, or a piece of guidance to help you more easily and consistently stay connected to your vision of what your life will look like once you've received the wealth you desire.

Card 3 indicates how to amplify the feeling of wealth.

This may be a mindset to shift into, an action to take, or something to reflect on that will allow you to amplify the feelings of having all the wealth you desire (before it physically manifests).

Card 4 indicates how holding the vision will pay off for you.

This is how holding the vision of your desired wealth per Cards 2 and 3 will begin to create ripple effects in your life—this may be abundance coming your way, new gifts you will gain access to that will help you bring more prosperity into your life, or opportunities that will be available to you.

Card 5 indicates what the universe wants you to know.

This is encouragement, wisdom, or advice from the universe to help you hold the vision and not become discouraged on your journey to the abundance you are embodying and moving toward.

"A HEARTFELT REQUEST CAN
OPEN THE FLOODGATES OF
ABUNDANCE."

Three things I already have that make me feel wealthy are...

Three things I can do right now that would make me feel wealthy are...

I want to let myself...

I would love to receive...

_____

_____

_____

_____

_____

_____

_____

_____

_____

_____

_____

_____

I want to ask the universe for...

_____

_____

_____

_____

_____

_____

_____

_____

Letting myself dream big here, what abundance do I desire to have in my wildest dreams? What is every single thing I desire to have?

_____

_____

_____

_____

_____

_____

_____

_____

_____

_____

_____

_____

_____

_____

_____

_____

_____

_____

_____

_____

_____

_____

What is a very detailed description of my next stage of abundance (one between where I am now and my big vision)?

*Does it feel good to think more about my **big** dreams of wealth? Or the next-level ones? Why? I know that either is valid and keeps me moving forward. I can hold the vision of whichever feels best to me at any time.*

MONEY MANTRAS FOR HOLDING THE VISION OF WEALTH

Choose one of the mantras below and repeat it 20 times. After doing so, reflect on what came up for you while reciting it.

The wealthier I feel, the wealthier I become.

When I dream big, the universe listens.

The wealth I desire is meant for me.

What were my experiences with this mantra? What thoughts, feelings, insights, or sensations did I experience?

_____
_____
_____
_____
_____
_____
_____
_____
_____
_____
_____
_____
_____
_____
_____
_____
_____
_____
_____
_____
_____
_____
_____
_____
_____
_____
_____
_____

"SHAPE YOUR EXPERIENCE IN THIS
LIFETIME WITH WORDS OF WEALTH."

Words of Wealth Activation

Words carry immense power. By speaking of what we desire (rather than what we fear or wish to avoid), we shape our worldview and claim the wealth we are moving toward. This practice allows us to create and identify opportunities for abundance that otherwise would have passed us by.

Use the following activation to speak your desired wealth into being. You are welcome to change the invocation that you read aloud in the activation for whatever you want. You can write a passage that details the exact vision for wealth that you hold— or even read your answers on some of the previous pages.

———————————

Take a few deep breaths to center yourself in the present moment.

Rest your attention on your neck and head. Envision a golden light filling your throat and mouth.

As you speak the following words aloud, feel this golden light infuse each word that leaves your mouth, imbuing them with abundance.

"With every breath, I grow more and more abundant.
With every word I speak, I create more and more wealth.

For my word is law, and what I say becomes my reality.

So I now declare that I am wealthy, all my desires are made manifest, and the vision of my abundance quickly becomes my lived experience.

And so it is."

Now that these words have been spoken, see them drift off into the universe, their golden light floating ahead of you and leading the way to the abundance you seek.

What were my experiences with this activation? What thoughts, feelings, insights, or sensations did I experience?

_____

_____

_____

_____

_____

_____

_____

_____

_____

_____

_____

_____

_____

_____

_____

_____

_____

_____

_____

_____

_____

When I speak of what I desire, I feel...

Some words that feel abundant to me are...

What story of wealth do I next want to speak into existence?

"BEFORE THE MONEY YOU DESIRE
CAN COME TO YOU, YOU MUST FIRST
BECOME THE WOMAN WHO FEELS
UNCONDITIONALLY WEALTHY."

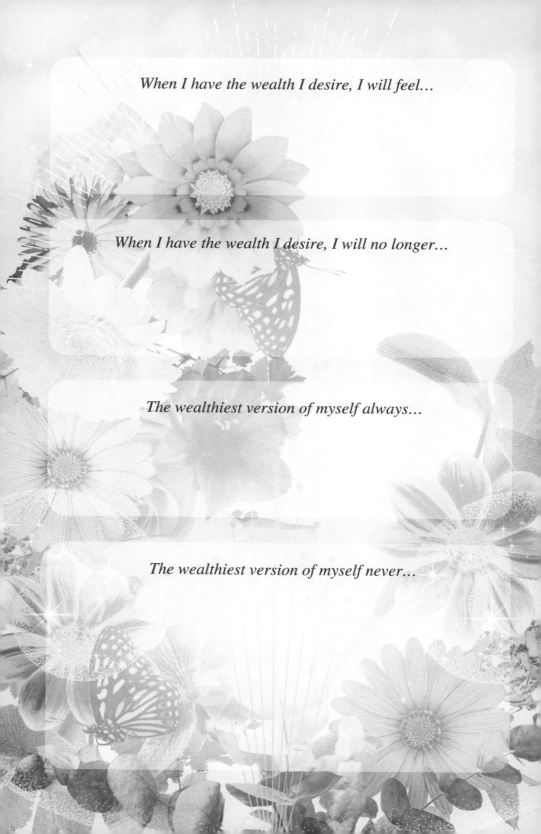

When I have the wealth I desire, I will feel...

When I have the wealth I desire, I will no longer...

The wealthiest version of myself always...

The wealthiest version of myself never...

How does the most abundant version of myself think?

_____

_____

_____

_____

How does the most abundant version of myself feel?

_____

_____

_____

_____

How does the most abundant version of myself act?

_____

_____

_____

_____

How can I begin to think, feel, and act more like this more abundant version of myself?

_____

_____

_____

_____

"RECONNECT WITH THE POSSIBILITY
FOR ABUNDANCE IN EACH MOMENT,
INCLUDING THIS ONE. THE MONEY YOU
DESIRE IS CLOSER THAN YOU THINK."

What are all the ways I can imagine more wealth coming into my life,
including ways different than how money typically comes to me?

_____

_____

_____

_____

_____

_____

_____

_____

_____

_____

_____

_____

_____

_____

_____

_____

_____

_____

_____

_____

_____

_____

What could happen in the next ten minutes that would make me feel incredibly wealthy? What are all the possibilities?

_____

_____

_____

_____

_____

_____

_____

_____

◆ ◆ ◆

_____

_____

_____

_____

_____

_____

_____

_____

_____

_____

MONEY MANTRAS FOR ABUNDANT POSSIBILITY

Choose one of the mantras below and repeat it 20 times. After doing so, reflect on what came up for you while reciting it.

Each moment holds limitless potential for abundance.

At any moment, more money may appear in my life.

Anything can happen at any time.

What were my experiences with this mantra? What thoughts, feelings, insights, or sensations did I experience?

_____
_____
_____
_____
_____
_____
_____
_____
_____
_____
_____
_____
_____
_____
_____
_____
_____
_____
_____
_____
_____

"THE GREAT SECRET TO CREATING
WILD ABUNDANCE IN YOUR LIFE IS THIS:

YOU MUST BECOME THE LIVING EMBODIMENT
OF THE ABUNDANCE YOU SEEK."

Others and the universe respond to the energy you carry and radiate. Your energy attracts prosperity to you.

The ability to feel as though you already possess the wealth you have in your vision is a superpower that you possess and can strengthen at any time. The more you embody the essence of your vision, the more quickly you create that reality around you.

Use the following activation to feel wealthy before the abundance you envision comes into your life (and to speed up the process of its appearance).

———————

Bring to mind the vision of wealth you wish to have.

Imagine what it will be like to have this reality be yours.

Now imagine that this reality is already yours.

What emotions, feelings, sensations, or energy arise within you as you imagine already possessing this wealth?

Pick the most positive feelings and notice where you feel this energy within your body.

Focus on that feeling, wherever it is in your body. As you do, allow the feeling to intensify.

Feel it grow, expanding to fill your entire body.

Sit with this energy, allowing it to grow greater and radiate out from you.

As you radiate out this energy of abundance, enjoy this feeling.

Memorize this feeling in your body.

Anchor in this energy.

Then hold this energy for as long as possible throughout your day, overflowing with the energy of wealth and bringing it to all that you do.

What were my experiences with this activation? What thoughts, feelings, insights, or sensations did I experience?

_____

_____

_____

_____

_____

_____

_____

_____

_____

_____

_____

_____

_____

_____

_____

_____

_____

_____

_____

_____

_____

_____

The energy of wealth feels like…

When I feel wealthy, I am inspired to…

"In this moment, you can be reborn, no longer being defined by memories that anchor you to your current financial reality.

See your limitless, unbridled potential as you are reborn into this moment."

At any moment, I can choose to look for…

I always have the ability to choose to feel…

*If I were to become the wealthiest version of myself
right now, I would…*

Prayer for Holding the Vision

Choosing to see yourself now as the future, wealthier version of yourself is how you create rapid transformation in your financial reality. It is impossible to see yourself differently and not change your thoughts, energy, and actions, which construct your financial reality. If you can *become* the wealthier version of yourself (in terms of how you see yourself and how you feel as you move through life) now, before the money shows up, you'll naturally find yourself moving toward that abundance faster than ever before. Use the prayer below whenever you want to transform into the wealthier version of yourself. You can see yourself however you want to see yourself now. You do not need to wait for the abundance you desire to become the version of yourself you've been wanting to become.

No longer will I wait to become the version of myself I want to become.

In this instant, I claim my power to step into being all that I can be.

I give myself permission to be everything I desire to be right now.

I now choose to see myself as the wealthiest, most fulfilled, most abundant version of myself.

I call upon the universe to help me remember my limitless potential and abundant nature.

Please help me to become the version of myself I desire to be in every thought, every breath, and every step.

I see my strength and celebrate it.

I know the wealth of my soul and am infinitely grateful for it.

I witness my own magic and am in awe of all that I am.

Today, I am reborn.

Today, I am—unconditionally and undoubtedly—the wealthiest version of myself.

Today, I become all that I am destined to become.

What were my experiences with this prayer? What thoughts, feelings, insights, or sensations did I experience?

_____

_____

_____

_____

_____

_____

_____

_____

_____

_____

_____

_____

_____

_____

_____

_____

_____

_____

_____

_____

_____

_____

What do I now give myself permission to think, feel, or do before the money I desire manifests in my life?

_____

_____

_____

_____

_____

_____

_____

_____

_____

_____

_____

_____

_____

_____

_____

_____

_____

_____

_____

_____

_____

_____

What version of myself do I now choose to become?

Parting Words

As you depart from this journal, I want to share two final thoughts with you.

First, I encourage you to revisit this journal in its entirety whenever you want to reach a new level of wealth. The messages are timeless, and you can delve deeper and deeper into them (and therefore increase your wealth) over time.

Second, I want to thank you. Truly, from the bottom of my heart and the most sacred parts of my soul, thank you for walking *The Way of the Wealthy Woman*. Thank you for sharing your light with the world and reconnecting with your innate power to create wealth in your life.

The more that we, as individuals, can positively transform our relationship with money, the more our society moves away from the old, limiting paradigms around it.

It's time for a new approach to money.

It's time for money to become an extension and reflection of the love we carry.

By transforming your experience of money, you are helping all of humanity to transform.

I am truly grateful to you for your contribution to the world, and I am honored to walk alongside you in *The Way of the Wealthy Woman*.

With love and abundance,
Taylor

Acknowledgements

This journal has the ability to transform lives—and the world—for the better. But it wouldn't be half as powerful without an entire team of people.

I am incredibly grateful for my publisher and artist, Stephanie Wicker-Campbell, for her ability to weave pure magic into images and elevate the messages in this journal far beyond what I envisioned.

I want to express my appreciation and thanks to my editor, Baylee Fox, for ensuring that the wisdom in this journal was communicated in the most powerful way possible.

I am unendingly grateful for my parents, who taught me to dream big and know my worth.

Thank you to my daughter, Ramona, who is far too young right now to realize how much she inspires me to keep pushing myself beyond the bounds of what I think is possible.

And to my husband, Dan, thank you for everything—truly—everything, including being the most wonderful partner, teammate, parent, and friend. Your constant belief in me has made everything I wanted—and more—possible. I have yet to find the right combination of words to express just how much I love you.

About the Author

Taylor Eaton is a pioneer in blending spirituality with financial empowerment. Her expertise lies in developing unique spiritual money tools that enable individuals to unlock financial abundance. Her multifaceted approach blends various modalities such as mindset work, meditation, Human Design, magick, oracle card readings, and more.

As an acclaimed money mindset expert, business mentor, and author of *The Wealthy Woman Oracle Deck*, Taylor's guidance has been instrumental in reshaping the financial reality for thousands of people. Her strategies are renowned for their holistic and personalized nature, catering to each individual's unique wealth journey. Taylor's philosophy centers on the conviction that everyone is entitled to a life of abundance and the spiritual tools they need to achieve it.

Outside of her professional achievements, Taylor cherishes the tranquility of nature and the simple joys of life. In her free time, she often finds solace hiking through the lush forests of the Pacific Northwest, accompanied by her husband, daughter, and their dogs.

Learn more about Taylor, her other works, ways to connect with her, and exclusive gifts for abundance by scanning the below QR code.